S0-AVO-804

WEEKLY WR READER®
EARLY LEARNING LIBRARY

WHY ANIMALS LOOK DIFFERENT

Animal Feet and Legs

Jonatha A. Brown

Reading consultant: Susan Nations, M.Ed., author/literacy coach/
consultant in literacy development
Science and curriculum consultant: Debra Voege, M.A., science
and math curriculum resource teacher

Please visit our web site at: www.garethstevens.com
For a free color catalog describing Weekly Reader® Early Learning Library's list
of high-quality books, call 1-877-445-5824 (USA) or 1-800-387-3178 (Canada).
Weekly Reader® Early Learning Library's fax: (414) 336-0164.

Library of Congress Cataloging-in-Publication Data

Brown, Jonatha A.
  Animal feet and legs / by Jonatha A. Brown.
    p. cm. — (Why animals look different)
  Includes bibliographical references and index.
  ISBN-10: 0-8368-6860-9 – ISBN-13: 978-0-8368-6860-9 (lib. bdg.)
  ISBN-10: 0-8368-6865-X – ISBN-13: 978-0-8368-6865-4 (softcover)
  1. Feet—Juvenile literature. 2. Leg—Juvenile literature. I. Title.
  II. Series: Brown, Jonatha A. Why animals look different.
  QL950.7.B76   2007
  573.9'9833—dc22   2006010996

This edition first published in 2007 by
Weekly Reader® Early Learning Library
A Member of the WRC Media Family of Companies
330 West Olive Street, Suite 100
Milwaukee, WI 53212 USA

Copyright © 2007 by Weekly Reader® Early Learning Library

Editor: Gini Holland
Art direction: Tammy West
Cover design and page layout: Charlie Dahl
Picture research: Diane Laska-Swanke

Picture credits: Cover, title, © Carol Walker/naturepl.com; p. 4 © Gary Carter/Visuals Unlimited;
p. 5 © Fritz Polking/Visuals Unlimited; pp. 6, 18 © Tom and Pat Leeson; p. 7 © Anup Shah/naturepl.com;
pp. 8, 15, 19 © Georgette Douwma/naturepl.com; p. 9 © Bob Newman/Visuals Unlimited; p. 10 © Mack
Henley/Visuals Unlimited; pp. 11, 14 © Michael H. Francis; pp. 12, 13 © Dave Watts/naturepl.com;
p. 16 © Joe & Mary Ann McDonald/Visuals Unlimited; p. 17 © Peter Blackwell/naturepl.com;
p. 20 © Lynn M. Stone/naturepl.com; p. 21 © John Waters/naturepl.com

Printed in the United States of America

1 2 3 4 5 6 7 8 9 10 09 08 07 06

Table of Contents

Cover and title page: Clydesdale horses have big feet with silky hair. Big feet help this Clydesdale gallop easily across the bumpy ground.

Run For Your Life!

In the world of animals, legs and feet come in many shapes and sizes. Deer have long legs that allow them to run fast. Cats have strong hind legs so they can pounce on their **prey**. Moles have short, strong front legs for digging.

This deer may be using its legs to save its life!

Monkeys use their feet to grip tree branches. Horses have hooves for running on hard ground. Hawks have claws for catching and holding small animals. Each kind of animal has the kind of legs and feet it needs to stay alive, or **survive**.

This hawk has caught a fish in its strong claws. Now the hawk holds the fish in its claws as it flies away.

Strong back legs help this tiger run in big leaps.

Running and Walking

Tigers, jaguars, and other big cats eat other animals. They are **predators**. Strong back legs are important to these cats. They need to run fast to catch their prey. Most cats also use their hind legs to leap onto their prey as the chase ends.

Both deer and antelope are prey animals. They try to run from big cats, wolves, and other predators. Deer and antelope have long legs so they can bound and run. Long legs help many prey animals run from danger.

This antelope needs long legs so it can run from animals that want to hurt it.

Flamingos can wade in deep water because they have long legs.

Flamingos wade in salty lakes to find shrimp to eat. Their long, slender legs let them move easily through the water. The flamingo's legs are longer than the legs of most other waders. This lets it wade in deeper water.

Camels have big, wide feet. They can walk on soft desert sand without sinking in. Snow leopards have big feet, too. Their feet have lots of fur between the toes. Their feet work almost like snowshoes. Furry feet keep the cat from sinking into deep snow.

These camels live in the sandy desert. Their big, wide feet keep them from sinking into the desert sand with each step.

The gibbon's front and back feet are shaped like hooks. This gibbon can hang from his back feet as well as from his front feet.

Swinging and Swimming

The white-cheeked gibbon is a small ape that spends most of its life in trees. Its legs and feet look like long arms with fingers. Gibbons can use their feet like hooks as they swing from one branch to another.

Beavers, frogs, and ducks spend lots of time in the water. They need to be good swimmers. All of these animals have webbed feet. They use their feet like paddles in the water. Webbed feet also keep these animals from sinking into soft mud.

A duck uses its wide, webbed feet to paddle across the water.

The kangaroo has short, small front legs and large, strong back legs. The kangaroo uses its back legs for hopping.

Hopping and Climbing

Kangaroos do not run. Instead, they use their long, strong hind legs for hopping. Rabbits and frogs also hop on their hind legs. These animals can hop on their hind legs as fast as many other animals can run on all four legs!

Tree frogs live in trees. Sticky pads on the bottoms of tree frogs' toes allow them to hold onto twigs and leaves. Raccoons spend most of their lives in trees, but they do not have sticky feet. Instead, they have strong claws for climbing.

Sticky pads help a tree frog hold onto a leaf with its toes.

This opossum uses its feet to get a good grip on a tree branch.

Gripping and Digging

Opossums are good climbers because their feet work like hands. Their hind feet have four toes that look like fingers. They also have one toe that looks like a thumb. These hand-like feet help opossums grip tree branches and vines.

All four feet of the koala are shaped like hands. Each front foot has three fingers and two thumbs! This gives the koala a strong grip.

This koala has wrapped all four of its feet around a branch. Now it can take a nap!

The Gila monster uses its sharp claws and strong front legs for digging.

The Gila [hee la] monster lives in the desert. It **burrows**, or digs, into the cool ground to get away from the desert sun. This lizard has short, strong front legs and long claws. These powerful legs and claws are good for digging.

Catching, Holding, and Fighting

Mountain lions and most other cats have sharp claws that help them catch and hold prey. Their claws slide back into their paws when they are not being used. We say they are **retractable**. This helps the cat's claws stay sharp.

This lion has caught a zebra in its claws. The big cat holds on tightly as the zebra tries to shake it loose.

Horses use their strong back legs and hard hooves for kicking. When two horses fight, they may even kill each other with their hooves.

Some animals use their feet for fighting. Ostriches have big feet with heavy claws. They use them to scratch and kick their enemies. Horses and zebras have hard hooves. A kick from any of these animals can hurt or even kill.

Some male crabs have one very large front claw. They fight by using this big claw as a club. When crayfish fight, they use their claws for grabbing. Sometimes they grab each other's legs and try to tear them off!

This male crab has one large claw and one small one. When male crabs fight, they hit each other with their large claws.

The Canadian lynx lives in places that have long, snowy winters. This kind of cat has lots of fur on its feet, which keeps its feet warm.

Fabulous Feet and Legs!

Feet can help animals stay both warm and cool. The Canadian lynx has very furry feet. This thick fur keeps its feet warm and dry in the snow. A dog's feet help it stay cool. Dogs sweat through their feet to cool off!

Legs and feet serve animals in many ways. Moles have short legs and long claws for digging. Zebras have long legs for running. Koalas have feet that work like hands for climbing and picking leaves. Each animal has the kind of legs and feet it needs to survive.

The mole's long claws and strong front legs help it dig a deep burrow. It can stay safe and warm in its burrow.

Glossary

burrows – digs

predators – animals that catch and eat other animals

prey – an animal that is killed and eaten by another animal

retractable – able to slide back into a protective covering

survive – live

For More Information

Books

Amazing Creatures. Eyes On Nature (series). Kidsbook Staff. (Kidsbook)

Animal Adaptations. (Life Science Library (series). Elizabeth Rose. (PowerKids Press)

Animals in Motion: How Animals Swim, Jump, Slither and Glide. Pamela Hickman. (Kids Can Press)

Animals on the Go. Jessica Brett. (Harcourt Childrens Books)

Web Sites

Creature World: Red Kangaroo
www.pbs.org/kratts/world/aust/kangaroo/index.html
Learn how far these animals can hop and more.

Mammal Word Search
www.apples4theteacher.com/mammalws.html
Find the hidden words in this online game.

Publisher's note to educators and parents: Our editors have carefully reviewed these Web sites to ensure that they are suitable for children. Many Web sites change frequently, however, and we cannot guarantee that a site's future contents will continue to meet our high standards of quality and educational value. Be advised that children should be closely supervised whenever they access the Internet.

Index

About the Author

Jonatha A. Brown has written many nonfiction books for children. She lives in Phoenix, Arizona, with her husband, Warren, and their two dogs, Sasha and Ava. Jonatha also has two horses, Fleetwood and Freedom. She would have more animals if Warren would only let her! They both enjoy watching coyotes, rabbits, ground squirrels, lizards, and birds in their backyard.